ESSENTIAL ELEMENTS
FOR UKULELE

COMPREHENSIVE UKULELE METHOD
MARTY GROSS

Playing the ukulele is an enjoyable, easy, and inexpensive way to get involved in music. It provides a way to learn musical concepts and skills that can apply to any instrument you decide to study. Moreover, it will give you a great opportunity to share the joy of making music with other people. This book will help to provide you with the basic skills and musical background you need to get started. Practice, experiment, and have fun playing the ukulele!

—*Marty Gross*

HISTORY OF THE UKULELE

In 1879, large numbers of Portuguese settlers traveled to the Hawaiian Islands to work on sugar cane plantations. Some of these workers brought along with them a love of music and a small guitar, called the braguinha, which were common in Portugal. Newspaper articles from the time describe how delighted the Hawaiian people were with the sound of these instruments. Among the emigrants, three skilled woodworkers, Manuel Nunes, Augusto Dias, and Jose do Espirito Santo, began to build stringed instruments. Changes were made to the design of these small guitars so that they would suit the tastes of the local Hawaiian musicians. The ukulele is the result of this combination of cultures.

The *'ukulele* (pronounced oo-koo-leh-leh) became extremely popular and quickly became part of the musical traditions of the Hawaiian Islands. When Hawaiian musicians performed at the World's Columbian Exposition in Chicago in 1893, interest in the ukulele spread across the mainland.

The ukulele has had several waves of popularity in the United States. In the 1920s and '30s, a lot of the sheet music for popular songs included ukulele chord symbols on the piano parts. Many well-known singers of the time used the instrument in their performances. The 1950s saw another rise in popularity for the ukulele, although by the mid-'60s, interest had shifted largely to the guitar as a sing-along instrument.

Since the late 1990s, the ukulele has gained popularity again. Players ("Somewhere Over the Rainbow") and Jake Shimabukuro have had popular hits that introduced a new generation to the ukulele.

T0079532

To access audio, visit:
www.halleonard.com/mylibrary
Enter Code
8881-6346-0334-0067

ISBN 978-1-4803-2169-4

HAL•LEONARD®

Visit Hal Leonard Online at
www.halleonard.com

Contact us:
Hal Leonard
7777 West Bluemound Road
Milwaukee, WI 53213
Email: info@halleonard.com

In Europe, contact:
Hal Leonard Europe Limited
42 Wigmore Street
Marylebone, London, W1U 2RN
Email: info@halleonardeurope.com

In Australia, contact:
Hal Leonard Australia Pty. Ltd.
4 Lentara Court
Cheltenham, Victoria, 3192 Australia
Email: info@halleonard.com.au

YOUR UKULELE

Sizes of Ukuleles

This book is written to be used with soprano, concert, or tenor ukuleles. The ukulele comes in four common sizes. The soprano, concert, and tenor all use the same tuning, which is called "C tuning" or "standard tuning." The strings are tuned to the notes G–C–E–A.

The larger baritone ukulele normally uses a different tuning called "G tuning." The strings are tuned to the notes D–G–B–E. This is the same as the four highest pitched strings of a guitar.

All of the ukuleles can be played together, but because of the difference in tuning, a baritone ukulele player will need to finger the notes and chords differently.

Soprano
(or "standard")

Concert

Tenor

Baritone

Parts of the Ukulele

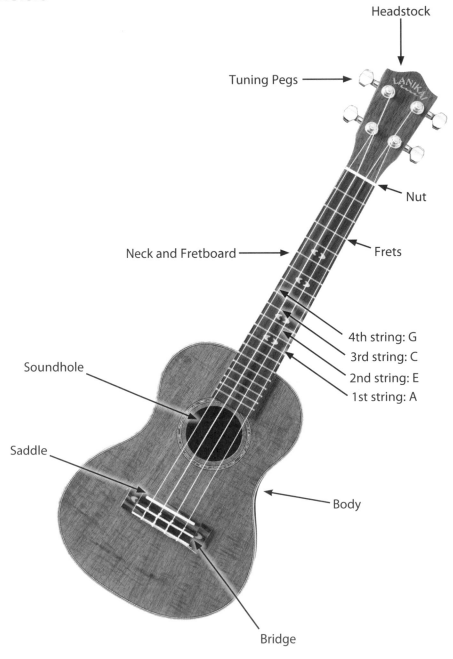

Headstock

Tuning Pegs

Nut

Neck and Fretboard

Frets

4th string: G
3rd string: C
2nd string: E
1st string: A

Soundhole

Saddle

Body

Bridge

GETTING STARTED

Playing Position

The best way for you to hold your ukulele will depend on the size of the instrument that you are using. Make sure that you are relaxed and sitting up straight, and then bring the instrument to you. Try these positions to see which works best.

- While resting the ukulele on your right leg, tilt the instrument to a comfortable angle so your left hand can move easily on the neck.

- If the ukulele is too small to rest on your leg, hold the instrument against your abdomen and cradle it with your right forearm. This is also the way you will hold a ukulele while standing.

Tuning

- Turning the tuning pegs will change the tension of the strings and thus change their pitch. As you increase tension, the pitch of the string will become higher. As you loosen the tension, the pitch will get lower.

- You may need only small adjustments to get in tune, so work in small steps.

- It is easier to start with a low sound and tune up to the pitch. If the pitch of the string is too high, loosen the string to lower the sound and then bring it up again gradually.

The ukulele is tuned as follows:

String 4: G
String 3: C
String 2: E
String 1: A

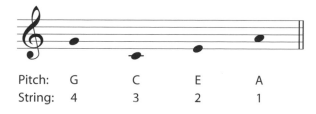

Pitch:	G	C	E	A
String:	4	3	2	1

Tuning to the Audio

The first audio track will play the pitch for each string, beginning with string number 4. While plucking the string, turn the tuning peg slowly until the sound of the string matches the sound on the recording.

To learn about other tuning methods, see page 45.

PLAYING CHORDS

Left-Hand Position

- For all diagrams in this book, left-hand fingers are numbered 1 through 4.
- Place your left thumb on the back of the ukulele neck.
- Keep your hand in a relaxed, rounded shape.
- Use the tips of your fingers to press the strings.

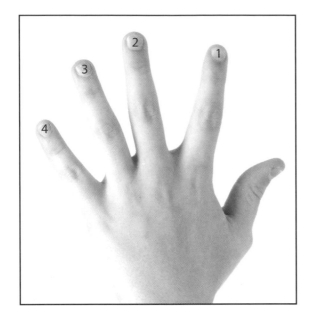

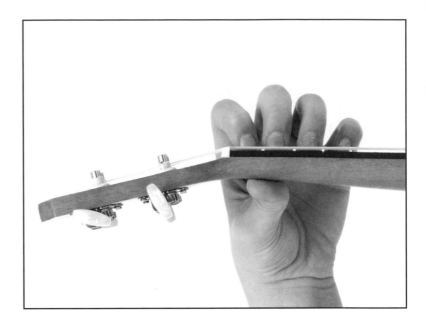

Understanding Chord Diagrams

A chord diagram is a map that shows you how to place the fingers of your left hand in order to play a particular chord.

Each numbered circle shows you where to depress a string and which finger to use.

In this example, you would:

- Use your first finger to press down the second string at the first fret.
- Use your second finger to press down the fourth string at the second fret.
- "O" above a string indicates an open string. The first and third strings are played open (unfretted) in this chord.

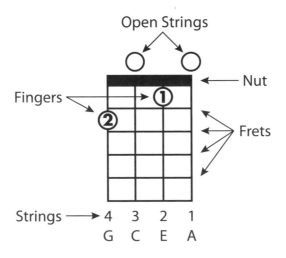

PLAYING CHORDS

Chords consist of three or more notes being played at the same time. Ukulele players often play chords to go along with singing. Press down the strings with the tips of your fingers. Strum by brushing your thumb in a downward motion across the strings. If your left-hand position is good, you will hear a clear tone from each of the four strings.

C Chord

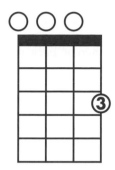

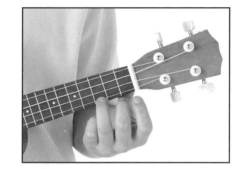

G7 Chord

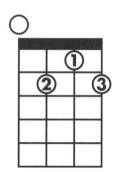

THEORY

Tempo   **Tempo** is the speed of the music.

STRUM BUILDER 1

Strum across all four strings in a smooth downward stroke. Each slash (/) stands for a single downward strum. Choose a tempo that allows you to change chords while keeping a steady beat. As you get used to changing the position of your left hand, you will be able to increase your speed.

1. STARTING OUT

C   G7   G7   C

/ / / /   / / / /   / / / /   / / / /

2. BABY STRUMS

C   G7   C   G7   C

/ / / /   / / / /   / /   / /   / / / /

PLAYING CHORDS

Let's use our two chords to strum and sing along with some familiar songs. Keep a steady, even tempo. As we move on, we'll be learning more about the musical symbols used here.

Learning to play any instrument well depends on learning how to practice. Throughout this book, you'll find tips on how to make the most of your practice time.

Practice Tip

Go through the following songs once to practice just the chord strumming, then go back and add the singing.

3. SKIP TO MY LOU

Traditional

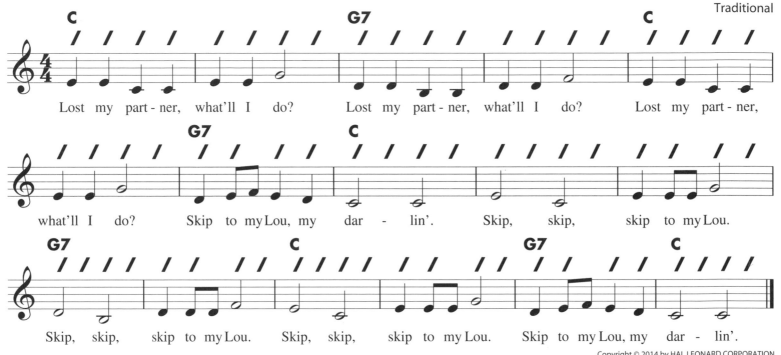

Lost my part-ner, what'll I do? Lost my part-ner, what'll I do? Lost my part-ner, what'll I do? Skip to my Lou, my dar-lin'. Skip, skip, skip to my Lou. Skip, skip, skip to my Lou. Skip, skip, skip to my Lou. Skip to my Lou, my dar-lin'.

4. HE'S GOT THE WHOLE WORLD IN HIS HANDS

Traditional Spiritual

He's got the whole world in His hands. He's got the whole world in His hands. He's got the whole world in His hands. He's got the whole world in His hands.

PLAYING CHORDS

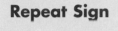
F
Chord

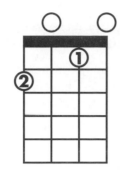

Repeat Sign

Without stopping, play once again.

5. THE LION SLEEPS TONIGHT   *Strum and sing this next song.*

New Lyrics and Revised Music by George David Weiss,
Hugo Peretti and Luigi Creatore

Verse 1:

Verse 2: (continue strum)

| C | F | C | G7 |

Near the village, the peaceful village, the lion sleeps tonight.

| C | F | C | G7 |

Near the village, the quiet village, the lion sleeps tonight.

To Chorus

Verse 3: (continue strum)

| C | F | C | G7 |

Hush, my darling, don't fear my darling, the lion sleeps tonight.

| C | F | C | G7 |

Hush, my darling, don't fear my darling, the lion sleeps tonight.

To Chorus

PLAYING CHORDS

STRUM BUILDER 2

Up to this point, you have always strummed in a downward motion. In music for stringed instruments, it's common to see that movement indicated using the downstroke symbol (⊓). You can also strum in an upward motion, which is indicated with an upstroke symbol (∨). Ukulele players use combinations of downstrokes and upstrokes to create different rhythms and styles of strums.

The strum pattern exercises below are written with music notation. For now, listen to the accompanying audio tracks or your teacher to get a feel for these rhythms. As you progress through the book, you'll learn more about how to read notation.

Practice the next exercise slowly until you get a steady, even sound on both strokes. Then try it more quickly. On the downstroke, use your thumb to strum the strings. On the upstroke, use the tip of your index finger to strum.

6. UPS AND DOWNS

Down   Down   Down   Down   Down   Up   Down   Up   Down   Up   Down   Up

7. CHANGE UP *Practice changing chords as you use your new strumming skills.*

Now that you can use both downstrokes and upstrokes, we can start to mix up combinations of rhythms in order to play different styles of music. Practice this strum, which we will use to play "Jambalaya" on the next page.

8. SUM OF EACH

PLAYING CHORDS

Use the strum you learned on the last page to play this song.

9. JAMBALAYA (On the Bayou)

Words and Music by
Hank Williams

PLAYING CHORDS

You can use the same strumming pattern to play this well-known folksong.

THEORY

Pick-Up Notes This song begins with three **pick-up notes**. Start the song by singing the first three words, "This land is…" and then begin strumming the F chord on "your."

10. THIS LAND IS YOUR LAND

Words and Music by
Woody Guthrie

Chorus:

This land is your land,_____ this land is my land,_____ from Cal - i -

for - nia_____ to the New York Is - lands;_____ from the Red - wood

for - ests_____ to the Gulf Stream wa - ter;_____

this land was made for you and me.

Verse 1: (continue strum)

    F   **C**
As I was walking that ribbon of highway

    G7   **C**
I saw above me that endless skyway;

    F   **C**
I saw below me that golden valley;

G7   **C**
This land was made for you and me.

To Chorus

Verse 2: (continue strum)

    F   **C**
I've roamed and rambled and followed my footsteps;

    G7   **C**
To the sparkling sands of her diamond deserts:

    F   **C**
And all around me a voice was sounding;

G7   **C**
This land was made for you and me.

To Chorus

HISTORY

Woody Guthrie (1912–1967) traveled America writing songs and performing as a singer and guitar player. The songs he wrote during the Great Depression and the Dust Bowl told the stories of hard times experienced by the poor, working people of our country. His songs remain an important part of our cultural history.

PLAYING CHORDS

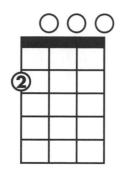

Am
Chord

STRUM BUILDER 3

We will create a new strum pattern by leaving one downward strum out of the pattern that you have used on pages 8–10. Your right hand will continue to move up and down in even rhythm. On the third downstroke, however, you will pass over the strings without strumming them.

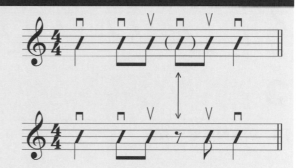

11. GIVE ME SOME SPACE *Practice this strum as you use the new A minor chord.*

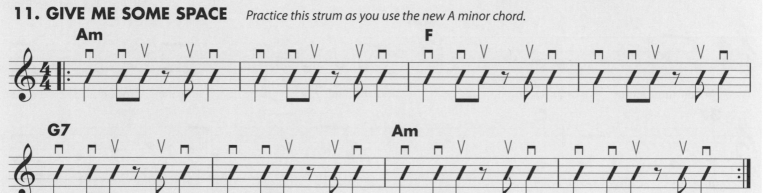

Practice Tip

Without strumming, name aloud each chord in the exercise above as you use your left hand to finger the chord formation. Notice that your second finger does not move when you change from Am to F. Also, your first finger stays in place when you change from F to G7.

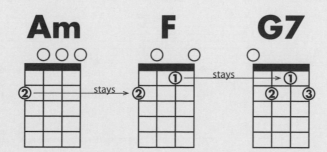

Try to keep the fingers of your left hand in place on the fretboard as much as possible. It will become easier to play chord changes when you eliminate extra movement, and it will create a smoother-sounding transition from chord to chord.

PLAYING CHORDS

Practice Tip

Use the strum you learned on the last page to play "Stand by Me." This song is based on a repeating chord pattern. Name the chords aloud as you practice the pattern; then go ahead and sing along with the chords.

12. STAND BY ME – Chord Pattern and Strum

13. STAND BY ME

Words and Music by Jerry Leiber,
Mike Stoller and Ben E. King

Using Your New Skills

Go back to page 7 and play "The Lion Sleeps Tonight" using the strum pattern that you learned here.

COUNTING

The Beat

The **beat** is the steady pulse of the music. Counting aloud and tapping your foot can help you to feel the beat. Tap your foot down on each beat as you count.

Count: **1** **&** **2** **&** **3** **&** **4** **&**
Tap: ↓ ↑ ↓ ↑ ↓ ↑ ↓ ↑

Notes

The shape of a **note** tells us how long to play each sound.

♩ = 1 Beat   Each **quarter note** will get one beat.

♩ = 2 Beats   Each **half note** will get two beats.

𝅝 = 4 Beats   Each **whole note** will get four beats.

14. THE COUNT   *Clap the rhythm as you count aloud.*

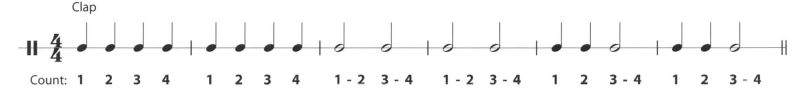

15. TAP 'N CLAP   *Now see if you can tap your foot on the beat as you clap and count.*

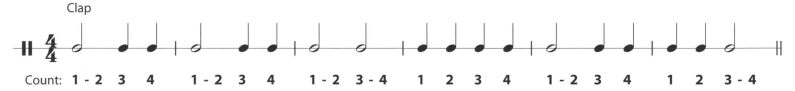

16. PICK IT UP   *Use your thumb to pick this rhythm on the open fourth string as you count.*

17. C THE RHYTHM   *Use your left hand to finger a C chord and strum this rhythm as you count.*

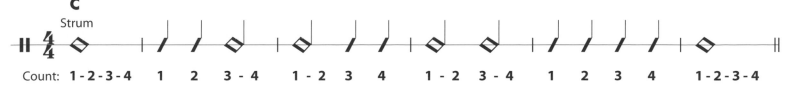

ESSENTIAL ELEMENTS QUIZ – Counting Notes   *Write in the number of beats that each note lasts.*

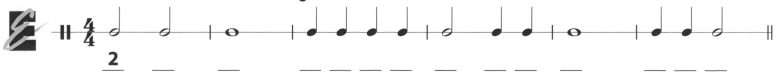

READING NOTES

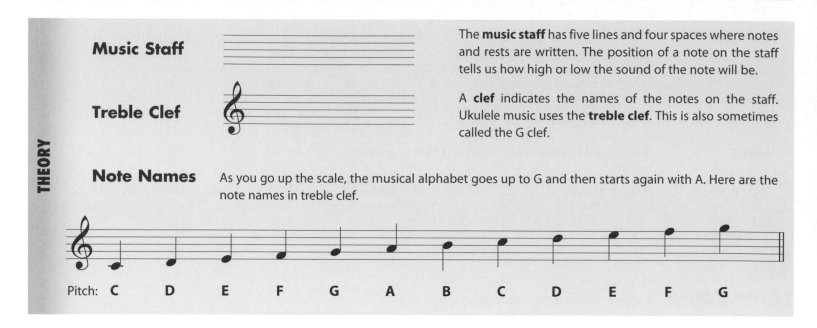

Music Staff — The **music staff** has five lines and four spaces where notes and rests are written. The position of a note on the staff tells us how high or low the sound of the note will be.

Treble Clef — A **clef** indicates the names of the notes on the staff. Ukulele music uses the **treble clef**. This is also sometimes called the G clef.

Note Names — As you go up the scale, the musical alphabet goes up to G and then starts again with A. Here are the note names in treble clef.

Pitch: C D E F G A B C D E F G

ESSENTIAL ELEMENTS QUIZ – Note Decoder

Use the staff above to write in the note names and spell these words. If you already know the notes of the treble clef, cover the staff above and write in the names from memory. Then check your work.

B _ _ _ _ _ _ _ _ _ _ _

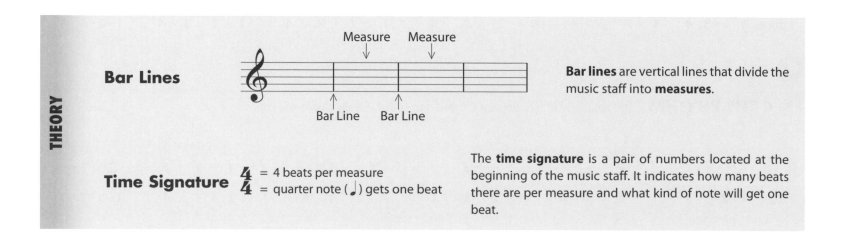

Bar Lines — Measure   Measure — Bar Line   Bar Line

Bar lines are vertical lines that divide the music staff into **measures**.

Time Signature — $\frac{4}{4}$ = 4 beats per measure
= quarter note (♩) gets one beat

The **time signature** is a pair of numbers located at the beginning of the music staff. It indicates how many beats there are per measure and what kind of note will get one beat.

NOTES ON THE THIRD STRING

Let's play some single notes. We'll begin on the third string and start to build a series of steps we can use to play melodies. We will only pick one string at a time. Pick the string with a downward motion of your thumb or use a hard felt pick.

C
Open

 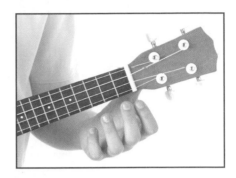

D
2nd Fret
2nd Finger

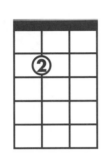 

18. BABY STEPS

19. FOUR OF A KIND

20. BACK AND FORTH

ESSENTIAL ELEMENTS QUIZ – Chord Review

Play this chord pattern for your teacher. Keep a steady beat and play one downward strum for each slash mark.

NOTES ON THE SECOND STRING

E
Open

E

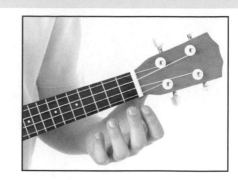

F
1st Fret
1st Finger

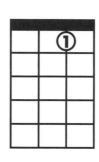

F

G
3rd Fret
3rd Finger

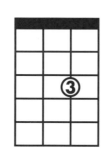

G

Play through the following exercises to get a feel for these new notes.

21. THREE STEPS CLOSER

22. ROUND AND ROUND

23. MILLARD FILLMORE'S INAUGURAL MARCH

PLAYING SINGLE NOTES

Using the five notes we have learned on the second and third strings, we can play many simple melodies.

24. STEP CLIMBER

25. GO TELL AUNT RHODY

Traditional

26. SKIPPING ALONG

27. ODE TO JOY

By Ludwig van Beethoven

ESSENTIAL ELEMENTS QUIZ – Note Review

Write in the names of the notes on the blanks beneath the line.

C

PLAYING CHORDS

G Chord

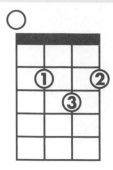

C7 Chord

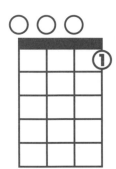

D7 Chord

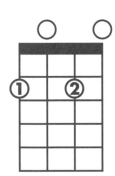

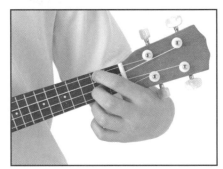

STRUM BUILDER 4

We will use this strum to play "Hound Dog" on the next page.

Practice Tip

Play the exercise below to practice your new chords and strum pattern. Listen to the audio track to hear the rhythm. Keep a slow, steady, walking tempo until you are changing chords easily.

28. WALKING THE DOG

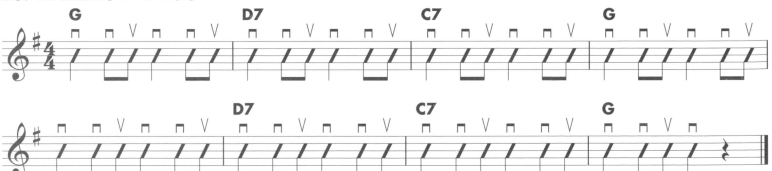

PERFORMANCE SPOTLIGHT

THEORY

N.C. The symbol **"N.C."** written above the staff stands for "No Chord." You should stop strumming, but continue singing, until you reach the next chord symbol.

Intro Many songs have an **introduction**, or **intro**. Found at the beginning of a song, it's an instrumental lead-in to the sung melody. An intro helps to establish the pitch, rhythm, and style of the song.

29. HOUND DOG *Strum and sing this classic Elvis hit.*

Words and Music by Jerry Leiber
and Mike Stoller

Copyright © 1953 Sony/ATV Music Publishing LLC
Copyright Renewed
This arrangement Copyright © 2014 Sony/ATV Music Publishing LLC
All Rights Administered by Sony/ATV Music Publishing LLC, 8 Music Square West, Nashville, TN 37203
International Copyright Secured All Rights Reserved

COUNTING RESTS

Rests Music is made up of both sound and silence. Just as the shape of a note tells us how long to hold a sound, the shape of a **rest** tells us how many beats of silence to count.

𝄽 = 1 Beat **Each quarter rest** will get one beat of silence.

▬ = 2 Beats **Each half rest** will get two beats of silence.

▬ = 4 Beats **Each whole rest** will get four beats of silence.

Practice Tip

For each exercise below, focus on the rhythm first. Count the beats aloud and clap the notes. Then go back and pick the melody in the proper rhythm.

30. FIRST QUARTER *Clap and count out loud.*

31. STAR POWER *Count aloud as you pick this melody.*

32. HALFWAY THERE

33. THE WHOLE DEAL

34. MIXING IT UP

NOTES ON THE FIRST STRING

It is time to add some single notes on the first string. First we'll practice just the new notes, A, B, and C, and then we'll add them to the notes you already know on the other strings.

A
Open

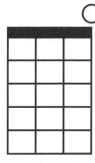

A

B
2nd Fret
2nd Finger

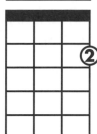
B

C
3rd Fret
3rd Finger

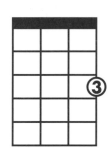

C

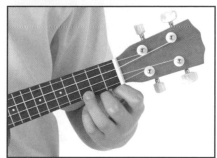

Practice Tip

Name each note out loud as you play it. It will help you to learn the note names and how the notes create patterns.

35. NEAR THE TOP

36. STEP LIGHTLY

37. SKIP A STEP

PLAYING NOTES

It's time to put together the notes you have learned on the 1st, 2nd, and 3rd strings.

38. ALL TOGETHER – C Scale

THEORY

3/4 Time Remember that the top number of a time signature indicates the number of beats in a measure, while the bottom number tells us what kind of note gets one beat. We will have three beats in each measure. A quarter note will get one beat.

39. SCALING THE HEIGHTS

THEORY

Tie

A **tie** is a curved line connecting two notes of the same pitch. Play one note for the combined counts of the tied notes.

40. WHEN THE SAINTS GO MARCHING IN

Traditional

Practice Tip

Have half of your group pick the melody of "When the Saints Go Marching In," while the other half strums the chords. For a simple strum, use two downstrokes in each measure.

PLAYING NOTES

Dotted Half Note ♩. A **dot** adds half of the value of the note. A dotted half note gets three beats.

♩ + ♩ = ♩.
2 Beats + 1 Beat = 3 Beats

41. AMAZING GRACE

Words by John Newton
From A Collection of Sacred Ballads
Traditional American Melody
From Carrell and Clayton's Virginia Harmony
Arranged by Edwin O. Excell

Flats ♭ A **flat** sign tells you to lower the pitch of a note by one half step. In this example, you would play a B♭.

B♭
1st Fret
1st Finger

B♭

42. ROCKIN' ROBIN

Words and Music by
J. Thomas

PLAYING NOTES

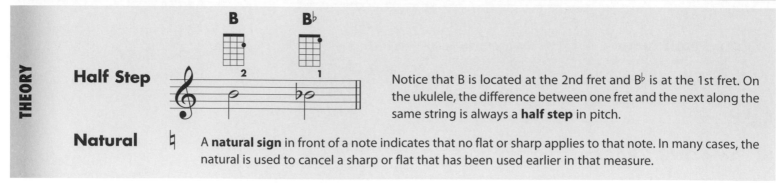

Half Step

Natural ♮ A **natural sign** in front of a note indicates that no flat or sharp applies to that note. In many cases, the natural is used to cancel a sharp or flat that has been used earlier in that measure.

Notice that B is located at the 2nd fret and B♭ is at the 1st fret. On the ukulele, the difference between one fret and the next along the same string is always a **half step** in pitch.

43. HALF-STEPPIN'

Key Signatures

The **key signature** at the beginning of a staff tells you that a flat or sharp will apply to the entire piece of music. In the key signature pictured here, every B that you play will be a B♭.

44. YANKEE DOODLE

Traditional

45. SIMPLE GIFTS

Traditional Shaker Hymn

PLAYING CHORDS

Barre Chords   Some chords require you to **barre** one finger across two or more strings. It may help to roll your index finger slightly so that you use the side of your finger. Take your time and listen carefully as you strum the chord to make sure that each string is sounding clearly.

B♭ Chord

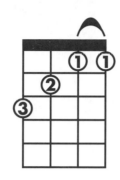

STRUM BUILDER 5

Use this strum for "You Are My Sunshine."

Using Your New Skills

Use what you have learned about note reading to find your starting pitch. Play just the first five notes of "You Are My Sunshine." It will show you what pitches to sing as you begin the song.

46. YOU ARE MY SUNSHINE

Words and Music by
Jimmie Davis

PLAYING CHORDS

Dm
Chord

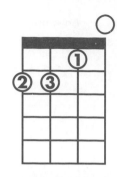

STRUM BUILDER 6

Use this strum for "Jamaica Farewell."

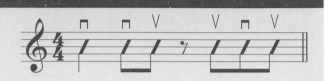

47. JAMAICA FAREWELL

Traditional Caribbean

1., 4. Down   the way where the   nights are gay ___ and   the   sun shines   dai - ly   on the
2. Sounds   of laugh - ter,   ev - 'ry - where, _ and   the   danc - ing   girls   sway-ing
3. Down at   the mar - ket,   you   can hear ___ la - dies   cry   out while on   their

moun - tain top, ___   I took a trip on   a   sail - ing   ship, _ and when I
to   and   fro, ___   I must de - clare _ my   heart is   there, _   though I've
heads   they bear ___   ac - kie, rice; _   salt   fish are   nice, _   and the

reached   Ja - mai - ca,   I   made a   stop. ___   But I'm   sad   to say   I'm
been   from Maine ___   to   Mex - i - co. ___   But I'm   sad   to say   I'm
sun   is warm_ an - y   time of   year. ___   But I'm   sad   to say   I'm

on my   way, _   won't be back   for   man-y a day. _   My heart is   down; _ my head is

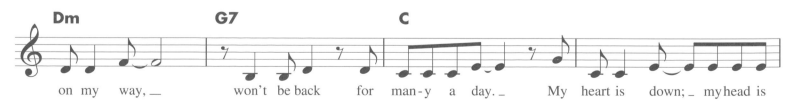

turn - ing   a - round. _   I had to   leave a   lit - tle girl   in   King - ston town. _

Play 4 times

PLAYING NOTES

Sharps ♯ A **sharp** sign tells you to raise the pitch of a note by one half step. In this example, you would play an F♯.

Just like flats, a sharp can be applied to one note or you can have a sharp in the key signature that applies to an entire piece of music. In the key signature pictured here, every F would be played as an F♯.

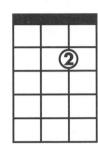

F♯
2nd Fret
2nd Finger

48. ONE SHARP GRANDPA

49. LOOK SHARP

Enharmonics are two notes that are written differently but sound the same. A piano keyboard provides a good way to both see and hear how this works. Each black key is both a sharp and a flat. For example, C♯ and D♭ are **enharmonic** to each other.

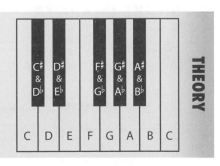

COUNTING

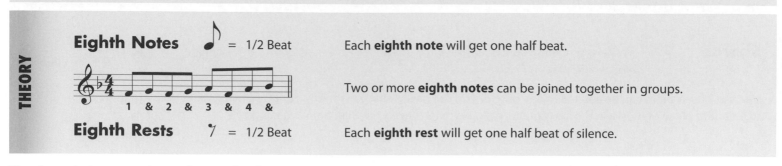

Play through these exercises and songs that feature the new eighth note. You've actually been playing eighth notes in your strum patterns since the beginning of the book.

50. 8TH-NOTE WORKOUT 1

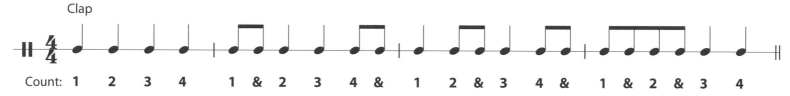

51. 8TH-NOTE WORKOUT 2

Practice Tip

You can clap the two exercises above as a duet. Divide your lesson group in half or work with a partner. Count aloud and clap the rhythm, and then switch parts.

52. SEA SHANTY

53. SNAKE CHARMER

PLAYING NOTES

Using Your New Skills

Go back to page 12 and pick the melody notes for "Stand by Me." Divide into groups or work with a partner. Play the chord strumming and the melody together.

THEORY

2/4 Time In **2/4 time**, we will have two beats in each measure. A quarter note will get one beat.

THEORY

54. LI'L LIZA JANE

Words and Music by
Countess Ada De Lachau

1st & 2nd Endings

A pair of numbered brackets above the staff indicates that there are two endings for the music. Play the 1st ending and repeat back to the beginning or to an earlier repeat sign if there is one. On the second time through, skip over the 1st ending and play just the 2nd ending.

THEORY

55. MICHAEL ROW THE BOAT ASHORE

Traditional Folksong

PERFORMANCE SPOTLIGHT

Choose a strum pattern to use with this song.

56. OCTOPUS'S GARDEN

Words and Music by Richard Starkey,
John Lennon and Paul McCartney

PLAYING CHORDS

Chord Review

The next two exercises contain all the chords you have learned so far. If you need to check a chord formation, look at the Chord Chart on pages 46 and 47.

57. CHORD REVIEW 1

58. CHORD REVIEW 2

Chord Challenge

The well-known folksong below, "On Top of Old Smoky," can be played using just three chords that you already know: C, F, and G7. Your challenge is to figure out the chord progression for the song. Here are the steps you should use:

1. Pick the first few notes of the melody so that you know the starting note on which to begin singing.

2. The blanks will tell you where you need to change chords. As you sing or hum the melody slowly, play one downstroke for each measure and experiment to see which chord (C, F, or G7) sounds good at each blank. Write in the chord names.

59. ON TOP OF OLD SMOKY

Kentucky Mountain Folksong

On top of Old Smok - y, _____ all cov-ered with snow, _____ I

lost my true lov - er _____ by a - court - in' too slow. _____

STRUM BUILDER 7

Now that you have worked out the chords for "On Top of Old Smoky," let's go back and use this three-beat strum to play the song. This Down-Up-Up strum creates the feeling of an old-fashioned waltz which fits nicely with the style of this folksong.

PLAYING CHORDS

F7 Chord

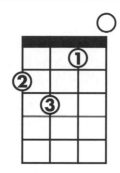

STRUM BUILDER 8

Use this strum for "Swing Low, Sweet Chariot."

60. SWING LOW, SWEET CHARIOT

Traditional Spiritual

READING TABLATURE

THEORY

Up to this point, we have been working on learning the symbols and vocabulary used in traditional music notation. We have used a five-line staff and a clef to tell us which notes to play. The basic ideas you have used while playing standard notation on the ukulele will apply to almost any other musical instrument that you decide to learn.

There is another method of writing music, called **tablature**, or **tab**, that is often used for instruments that have a fretted fingerboard, such as the ukulele, guitar, or banjo. Tablature is a map that shows you where to place your fingers on the fretboard in order to play the correct pitches. You may see tab used alone, or it may be connected to a traditional staff.

Each of the four horizontal lines of the tablature staff represents one string on your ukulele.

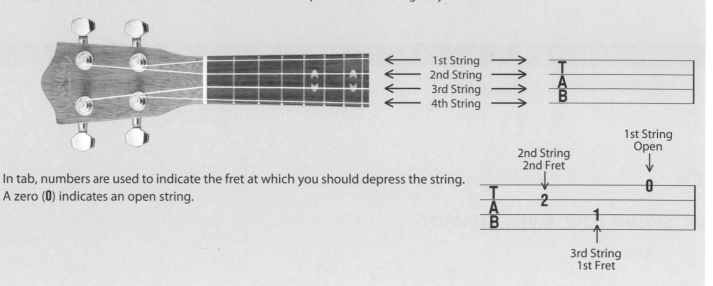

In tab, numbers are used to indicate the fret at which you should depress the string. A zero (**0**) indicates an open string.

Let's see how some musical lines you already know would look written in tablature. Follow the tab as you play each example.

61. C SCALE - Tab

62. ROCKIN' ROBIN - Tab

Words and Music by
J. Thomas

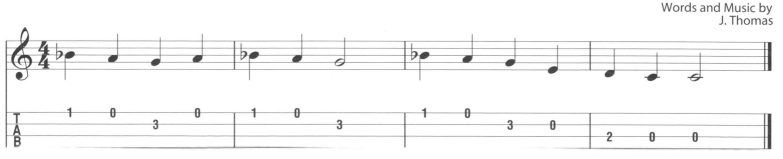

READING TABLATURE

Play these new exercises by reading the tablature.

63. SHORTENIN' BREAD

Traditional

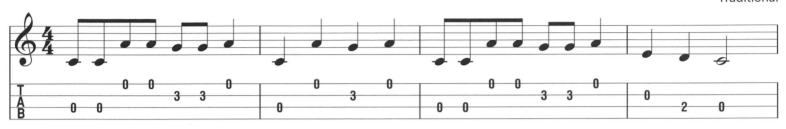

64. FRÉRE JACQUES (Are You Sleeping?)

Traditional

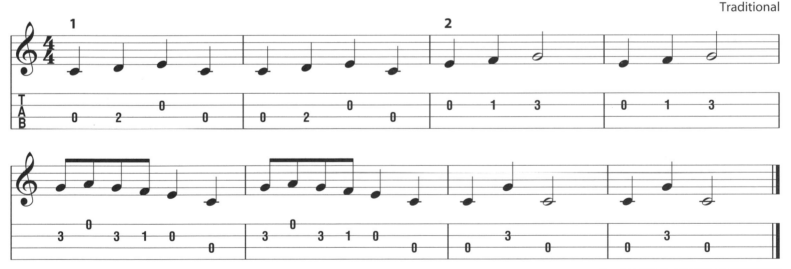

Practice Tip

Once you can play "Frère Jacques" by yourself, work with a partner and play the song as a round. The second player should begin after the first player has completed two measures (see numbers above staff).

QUIZ – Tab, You're It! *Write in the correct tab numbers for this melody.*

PLAYING CHORDS

A7
Chord

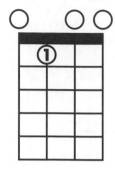

STRUM BUILDER 9

Use this strum for "Take Me Out to the Ball Game."

65. TAKE ME OUT TO THE BALL GAME

Words by Jack Norworth
Music by Albert von Tilzer

PLAYING MOVEABLE CHORDS

There are several ways to play each chord on the ukulele. We have been learning the most basic, commonly used chord formations. Different formations of the same chord will give you slightly different sounds and may make moving between chords on the fretboard easier. Because there are just four strings on the ukulele, players often use **moveable chords**. These shapes are set formations of your fingers that can be moved up and down the fretboard to produce a series of chords. Any chord shape that presses down all four strings can be moved to any fret.

You already know one moveable chord. Take a look at the B♭ chord that we have been using throughout this book. Since we hold down every string, we can move this shape up the fretboard to play other chords.

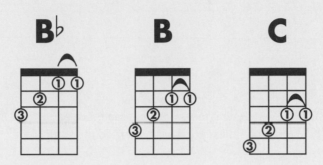

Each time we move up by one fret, the chord is one half step higher.

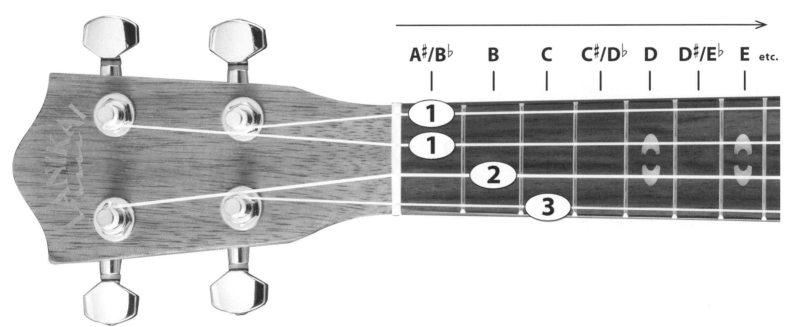

Practice Tip

Play the moveable B♭ chord shape. Slowly move up, one fret at a time, listening carefully to make sure you are keeping a good left-hand position. Name each chord out loud as you move the formation. Work as far up the fretboard as you are comfortable and able to maintain good tone.

Play the moveable C chord.

Listen closely and compare the sound to the simple C chord we have been using since the beginning of the book. Both are correct, but depending on the song you are playing, one might sound better than the other.

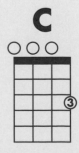

PLAYING MOVEABLE CHORDS

The song "La Bamba" gives us a good chance to try using a moveable chord shape. The song uses only three chords: F, B♭, and C. We will use the same shape for B♭ and C. Just move the B♭ formation up two frets to play C.

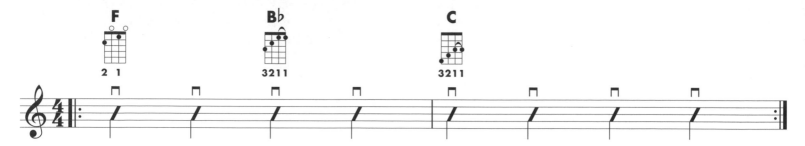

Practice Tip

Practice the pattern above with steady, even downstrokes until you can move easily from B♭ to C. Then play through "La Bamba" with this simple strum. We will add a more complicated strum pattern to the song later.

66. LA BAMBA

By Ritchie Valens

Lyrics under the staves:

- ba. Ar - ri - bay ar - ri - ba. Por ti se - re,

—— por ti se - re, por ti se - re. Yo no soy ma - ri -

ne - ro. Yo no soy ma - ri - ne - ro, soy ca - pi - tan;

—— soy ca - pi - tan, —— soy ca - pi - tan. ——

Chorus

Bam - ba, bam - ba. Bam - ba, bam - ba.

Bam - ba, bam - ba. Bam - ba, bam - ba!

Ritchie Valens (1941–1959) was a Mexican-American singer, songwriter, and guitar player. He combined traditional Hispanic music with the early sounds of rock 'n' roll. The popularity of his songs introduced many people to the musical sounds of another culture.

 HISTORY

STRUM BUILDER 10

Practice this strum pattern and then go back and play "La Bamba" using this rhythm.

PLAYING MOVEABLE CHORDS

Here's another useful moveable chord formation. It's another way to play the D7 chord. This chord shape requires you to barre across three strings with your first finger.

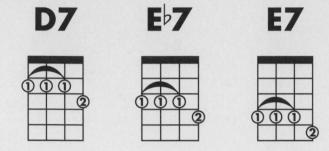

Like any moveable chord, this shape can be moved to any fret on the fingerboard. Each time you move up one fret, the chord will be one half step higher.

Using Your New Skills

Use the moveable D7 formation and the strum you learned on page 11 to play the calypso style of the Caribbean song, "Marianne."

67. MARIANNE

Traditional

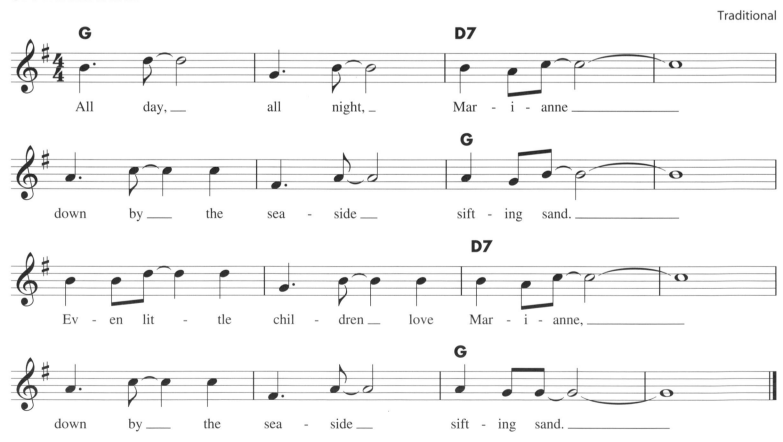

All day,— all night,— Mar - i - anne _____

down by ___ the sea - side ___ sift - ing sand. _____

Ev - en lit - tle chil - dren ___ love Mar - i - anne, _____

down by ___ the sea - side ___ sift - ing sand. _____

Calypso is a style of Afro-Caribbean music that began in Trinidad and Tobago. In the 1950s, the singer Harry Belafonte was important in bringing the sound of this musical style to the United States. The musical heritage of the Caribbean Islands became a familiar sound in America due to his popular recordings.

PLAYING CHORDS

Chord Challenge

"Home on the Range" can be played using three chords that you already know: G, C, and D7. Use your note reading and chord skills to figure out the chord changes. Write the correct chord names in the blanks.

68. HOME ON THE RANGE

Lyrics by Dr. Brewster Higley
Music by Dan Kelly

PLAYING CHORDS

Em Chord

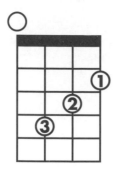

E7 Chord

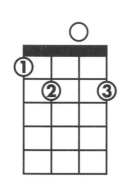

STRUM BUILDER 11

Use this strum for "The Rainbow Connection."

Notice there's another new chord in this tune: the D chord. Check out the Chord Chart on page 46 to learn this one. It is similar to the D7 and Dm chords you already know.

69. THE RAINBOW CONNECTION (from *The Muppet Movie*)

Words and Music by Paul Williams
and Kenneth L. Ascher

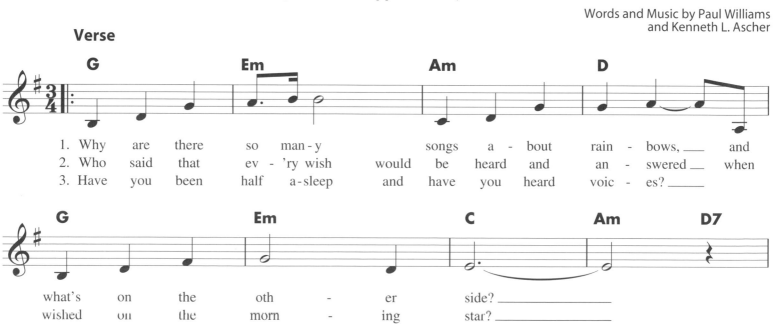

1. Why are there so man-y songs a-bout rain-bows, ___ and
2. Who said that ev-'ry wish would be heard and an-swered __ when
3. Have you been half a-sleep and have you heard voic-es? _____

what's on the oth - er side? _____
wished on the morn - ing star? _____
I've heard them call - ing my name. _____

PERFORMANCE SPOTLIGHT

G♯+
Chord

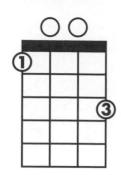

The plus symbol (+) in a chord name
indicates an augmented chord.

70. ALL MY LOVING *Look at the Strum Chart on page 48 and choose a strum pattern to use with this song.*

Words and Music by John Lennon
and Paul McCartney

Verse

Dm   G7   C   Am

1. Close your eyes and I'll kiss ___ you. ___ To-mor-row ___ I'll miss ___ you; ___ re-
(2.) tend that I'm kiss-ing ___ the lips I ___ am miss-ing ___ and

F   Dm   B♭   G7

mem-ber ___ I'll al-ways ___ be true. ___
hope that ___ my dreams will ___ come true. ___   And then

Dm   G7   C   Am

while I'm a-way, ___ I'll write home ev-'ry day ___ and I'll

1.
F   G7   C   N.C.

2.
C

send all my lov-ing ___ to you. ___ 2. I'll pre-   you. ___

Chorus

N.C.   Am   G♯+   C

___ All my lov-ing ___ I ___ will send to you, ___ all ___ my

Am   G♯+   C

lov-ing ___ dar-ling, I'll ___ be true. ___

TUNING METHODS

Electronic Tuners

Electronic tuners analyze a pitch and display whether the sound that you are playing is sharp, flat, or in tune. There are many options by a variety of makers. Tuners that clip directly on the headstock of the ukulele are easy to use and have become quite popular.

Learning to hear pitches and tuning by ear are important basic skills that every musician needs to develop. Electronic tuners can be a useful tool to help you check your tuning. Practice tuning by ear first, and then check your pitches against the tuner. As time goes on, you will find that your ability to tune by ear will become more and more accurate.

Keyboard

Similar to the way we have used the first audio track, you can tune by matching the pitch of any other instrument that is correctly tuned. A piano or electronic keyboard is a good reference for in-tune pitches.

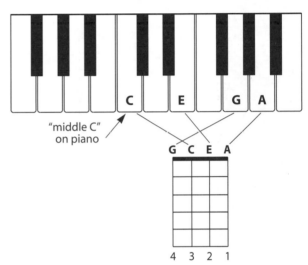

Relative Tuning

You can use relative tuning to make sure the strings of the ukulele are properly in tune with each other. This is a good way to quickly check your tuning.

- Assume that the third string is properly tuned to C.
- Play an E by pressing the third string at the fourth fret. Adjust the open second string to match that pitch.
- Play an A by pressing the second string at the fifth fret. Adjust the open first string to match that pitch.
- Play a G by pressing the third string at the seventh fret. Adjust the open fourth string to match that pitch.

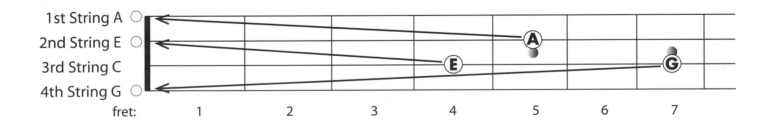

CHORD CHART

As you learn new songs on your own, you will encounter chords that were not used in this book. You can use this chart to find the formations for many of those new chords. The chart includes the major, minor, and dominant seventh chord for each step of the scale.

	MAJOR	MINOR	DOM7
C	**C**	**Cm**	**C7**
C♯/D♭	**C♯/D♭**	**C♯m/D♭m**	**C♯7/D♭7**
D	**D**	**Dm**	**D7** **D7**
D♯/E♭	**D♯/E♭**	**D♯m/E♭m**	**D♯7/E♭7**
E	**E**	**Em**	**E7**
F	**F**	**Fm**	**F7**

	MAJOR	MINOR	DOM7
F♯/G♭	F♯/G♭ 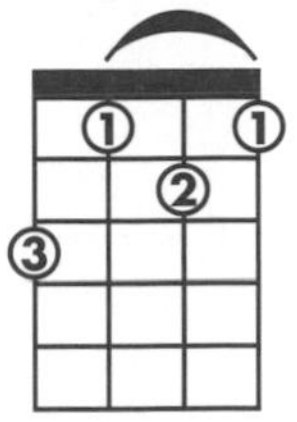	F♯m/G♭m 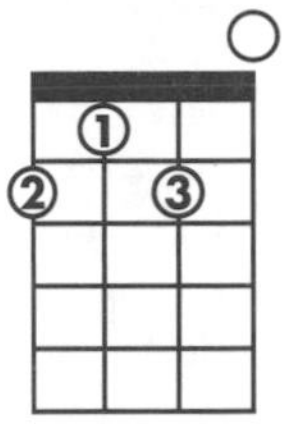	F♯7/G♭7 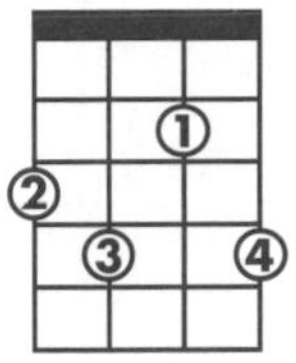
G	G 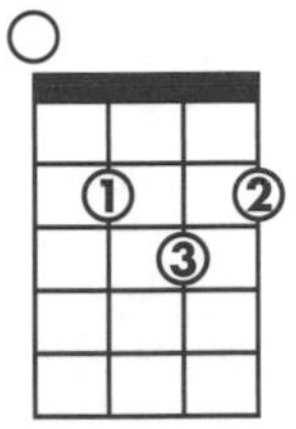	Gm 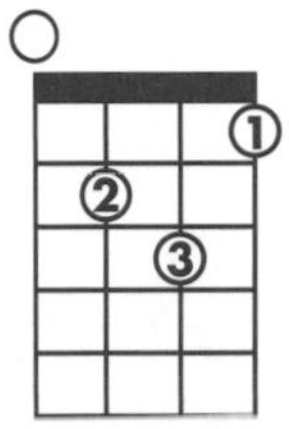	G7 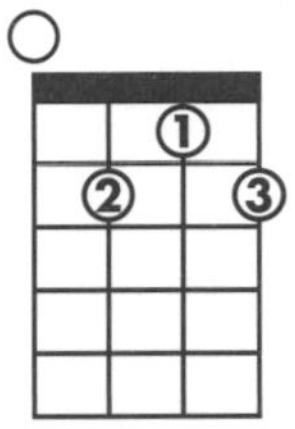
G♯/A♭	G♯/A♭ 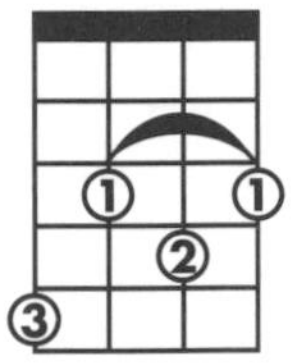	G♯m/A♭m 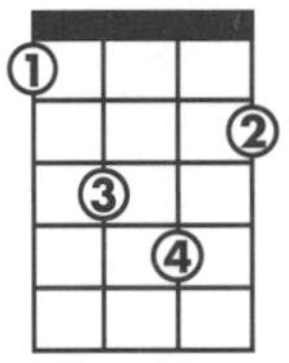	G♯7/A♭7 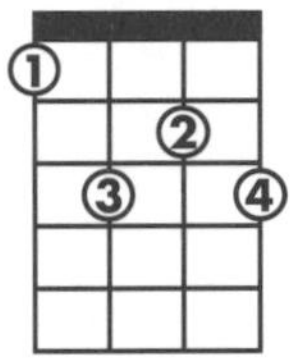
A	A 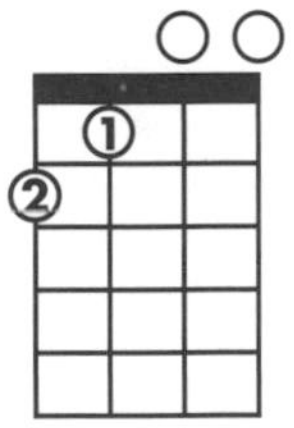	Am 	A7 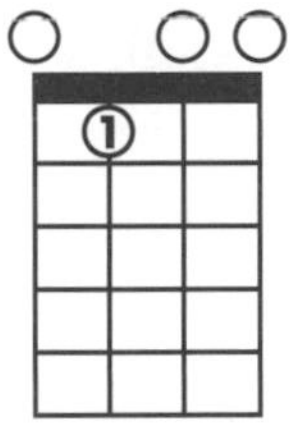
A♯/B♭	A♯/B♭ 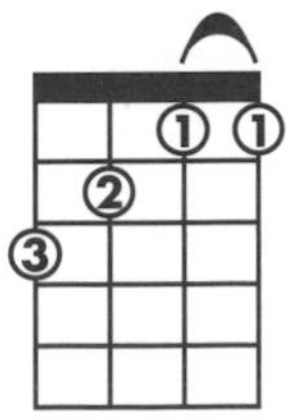	A♯m/B♭m 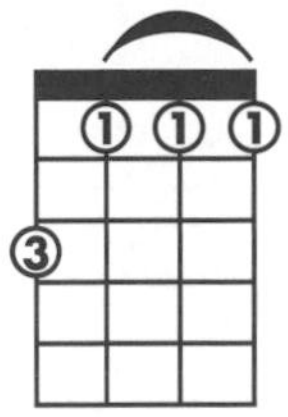	A♯7/B♭7 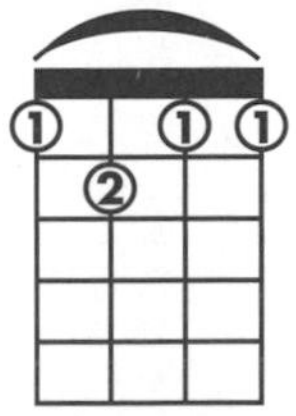
B	B 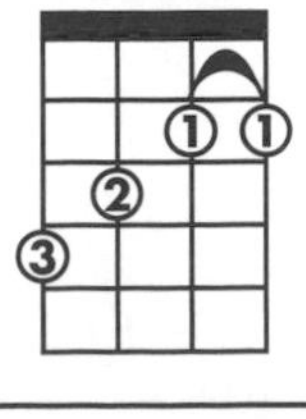	Bm 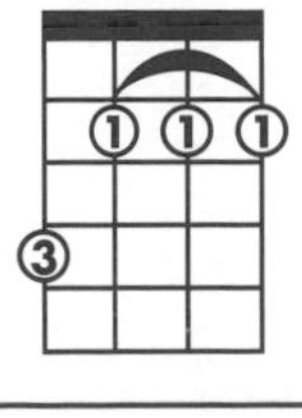	B7 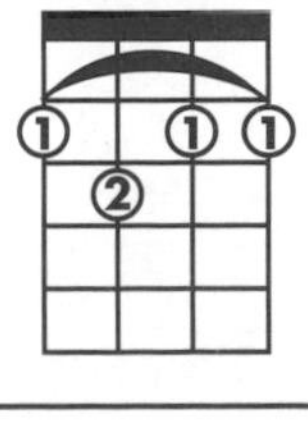

STRUM CHART

Here are the strum patterns that we have used throughout the book. As you learn new songs, it may help to refer back to these rhythms. As your playing skills progress, you will continue to develop more complicated strum patterns to match the styles of the songs you play. Listening to good ukulele and guitar players will give you helpful ideas for your own playing.